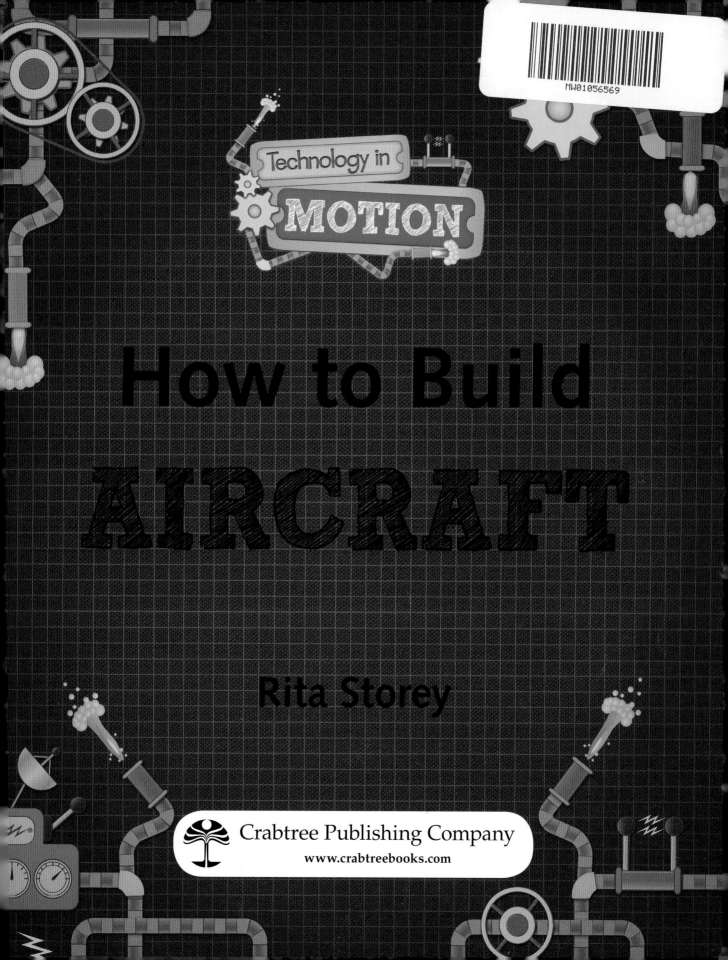

Technology in
MOTION

How to Build
AIRCRAFT

Rita Storey

Crabtree Publishing Company
www.crabtreebooks.com

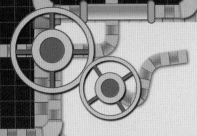

Crabtree Publishing Company
www.crabtreebooks.com
1-800-387-7650

Published in Canada
Crabtree Publishing
616 Welland Avenue
St. Catharines, ON
L2M 5V6

Published in the United States
Crabtree Publishing
PMB 59051
350 Fifth Ave, 59th Floor
New York, NY 10118

Published in 2017 by CRABTREE PUBLISHING COMPANY.

First published in 2016 by The Watts Publishing Group
(A division of Hachette Children's Books)
Copyright © The Watts Publishing Group 2016

Author: Rita Storey

Editorial director: Adrian Cole

Project coordinator: Kathy Middleton

Editor: Petrice Custance

Design manager: Peter Scoulding

Cover design and illustrations: Cathryn Gilbert

Proofreader: Wendy Scavuzzo

Prepress technician: Samara Parent

Print and production coordinator: Katherine Berti

The publisher would like to thank the following for their kind permission to reproduce their photographs:

Billyhill: (middle right), Chowells: 4 (bottom), Cpl Andy Benson/RAF; Cpl Lee Goddard/RAF: p5 (middle left); Juan Lacruz: 4 (top); Library of Congress: (middle right); Mike Peel: 4 (middle); Mike Young at English Wikipedia; (top right); Mitruch: 4 (middle); ReptOn1x: 15 (bottom); Trev M: (bottom left); US Air Force (middle right, bottom right); US Oceanic and Atmospheric Administration (bottom right);

Step-by-step photography by Tudor Photography, Banbury.

Every attempt has been made to clear copyright. Should there be any inadvertent omission, please apply to the publisher for rectification.

The website addresses (URLs) included in this book were valid at the time of going to press. However, it is possible that contents or addresses may have changed since the publication of this book. No responsibility for any such changes can be accepted by either the author or the Publisher.

Printed in Hong Kong/012017/BK20171024

Library and Archives Canada Cataloguing in Publication

Storey, Rita, author
    How to build aircraft / Rita Storey.

(Technology in motion)
Issued in print and electronic formats.
ISBN 978-0-7787-3384-3 (hardback).--
ISBN 978-0-7787-3395-9 (paperback).--
ISBN 978-1-4271-1906-3 (html)

    1. Airplanes--Design and construction--Juvenile literature. 2. Airplanes--Models--Design and construction--Juvenile literature.I. Title.

TL547.S76 2016   j629.133'34   C2016-906627-4
                                          C2016-906628-2

Library of Congress Cataloging-in-Publication Data

Names: Storey, Rita, author.
Title: How to build aircraft / Rita Storey.
Description: New York, NY : Crabtree Publishing Company, 2017.
Series: Technology in motion | "First published in 2016 by The Watts Publishing Group." | Audience: Ages 10-14. | Audience: Grades 7 to 8. | Includes index.
Identifiers: LCCN 2016045809 (print) | LCCN 2016048980 (ebook) | ISBN 9780778733843 (hardcover) | ISBN 9780778733959 (pbk.) | ISBN 9781427119063 (Electronic book text)
Subjects: LCSH: Airplanes--Design and construction--Juvenile literature. | Airplanes--Models--Design and construction--Juvenile literature.
Classification: LCC TL671.2 .S784 2017 (print) | LCC TL671.2 (ebook) | DDC 629.133/34--dc23
LC record available at https://lccn.loc.gov/2016045809

Contents

SAFETY FIRST

Some of the projects in this book require scissors, sharp tools, or a hot glue gun. We recommend that children be supervised by a responsible adult for the undertaking of each project in this book.

Flying machines

Have you ever wondered how people learned to build flying machines?

For centuries, people tried to copy the way birds fly, sometimes by attaching human-made wings to their bodies and flapping them! This, of course, was unsuccessful, but eventually engineers found ways to become airborne.

Gliding and floating

Gliders, paragliders, and hang gliders are flying machines that bring humans as close as they can get to bird flight. These machines have no power source, so they glide through the air silently, riding on currents of air.

These flying machines stay up in the air because air moves faster over the top of their angled wings than beneath them, causing higher pressure that results in **lift**. With no power source to generate **thrust**, these flying machines have to start their journey from a high place or be towed into the air and launched.

Hot-air balloons float up because the hot air trapped inside them is lighter than the colder air surrounding them.

Powered flight

Adding an engine and a propeller to a winged flying machine allows it to generate thrust and take off into the air under its own power. Add a jet engine to an airplane and you are really going places! Engineers design airplanes to suit their intended use. The Spitfire's wing shape (left) and powerful engine gave pilots a plane with the ability to make tight turns during the Second World War (1939–1945).

Civil aviation

Every day, all around the world, airplanes transport passengers and cargo over short and long distances. Air traffic controllers track the movement of planes that are in the air, guiding pilots safely through busy international airspace. These planes vary in size from the eight-seater Britten-Norman Islander, designed for short hops between islands, to the monster Airbus A380 (right), which can carry up to 853 passengers on international flights.

Aircraft at war

The demands of war have boosted the development of aircraft design from the earliest days. Some aircraft, including Chinook helicopters (left), are used to carry troops and equipment. While others, such as the B-2 Spirit (below), are designed to fly undetected on spying missions. In battle, fast fighter planes are used for air-to-air combat, and bomber aircraft carry bombs or missiles.

Drones

Unmanned Aerial Vehicles (UAVs), usually known as drones, are controlled remotely by a crew on the ground. These pilotless vehicles are used for gathering information, as well as for dropping bombs.

The American-made Predator UAV (right) was the first military drone. It could fly for as long as 40 hours at altitudes of up to 24,934 feet (7,600 m) on **reconnaissance** or deadly bombing missions.

Engineers are always searching for new ways to design aircraft. The Boeing X-51A WaveRider (left) has traveled at **hypersonic** speeds of almost 4,000 mph (6,437 kph).

Before you get started on each of the projects in this book, you'll need to gather together the materials and tools listed in the "you will need" box. Hopefully you will have most things on hand, but some of the more unusual items can be found in most hobby or craft stores.

Hot-air balloon

Watch your very own hot-air balloon float up into the sky!

Why does this happen? The hot air inside the balloon is lighter than the cold air all around it. When the air inside the balloon cools down, it will sink back down to the ground.

To make the hot-air balloon, you will need:
- 2 large, thin garbage bags
- tape
- paper or plastic cup
- scissors • ruler
- 4 12-inch (30 cm) lengths of string

1

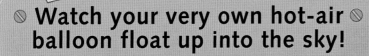

Cut the bottom off one garbage bag so it forms a tube. Tape it to the open end of the second garbage bag. Make sure there are no gaps where air could escape when the garbage-bag balloon is being filled with hot air.

2

Tie four knots in the open end.

3

2 inches (5cm)

Cut the bottom 2 inches (5 cm) off the paper cup. Carefully use the point of the scissors to make four holes equally spaced around the edge of the paper cup.

4

Tie one end of each length of string through the holes in the paper cup.

5

Tie the other end of each string onto a knot on the garbage-bag balloon.

6

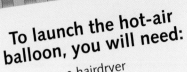

To launch the hot-air balloon, you will need:

- hairdryer
- access to a plug socket
- paper and pen to record what happens

6

Put the nozzle of the hairdryer through the opening at the bottom of the garbage-bag balloon. Turn the hairdryer on and wait until the balloon is full of hot air. Watch your hot-air balloon float up into the air!

A fair test

Try making these adjustments to the hot-air balloon. Make one change at a time.

- What happens if you make a bigger balloon?
- How far does the balloon travel if you place a toy passenger in the paper-cup basket?
- What happens if you use a different type of garbage bag?

Aircraft science

To design aircraft, you must understand the four forces that affect an aircraft while it is flying. In an ideal design, all four forces are evenly balanced.

Lift is the force that keeps an airplane in the air. It occurs because a plane's wings form a special shape called an **airfoil**, which uses air currents to generate a pushing force from below the wings. For more on this, read about Bernoulli's Principle at the bottom of this page.

Drag is the force of resistance that tries to stop an airplane from moving through the air. **Friction** causes drag. Good airplane design minimizes drag.

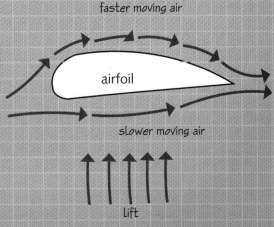

Thrust is the forward movement of an airplane. This can be generated by a rocket engine or by rotating propeller blades powered by the plane's engines.

Gravity is the force that pulls an airplane down toward Earth. Lightweight materials will help fight against the pull of gravity.

Aerodynamics

The way that air moves around objects is called aerodynamics. It is an important factor in airplane design.

Bernoulli's Principle

Engineers use Bernoulli's Principle, named after Swiss mathematician Daniel Bernoulli, to design aircraft. The principle explains the relationship between aircraft wing shape and the pushing force, or lift.

Most aircraft wings are rounded at the top and flatter at the bottom, forming an airfoil. As the aircraft moves forward, its wings push through the air. The air moving over the top of the wings moves a little faster than the air traveling underneath the wings, creating lower air pressure on top of the wings and higher air pressure beneath the wings. This pushes the aircraft up into the air—the force called lift.

faster moving air

airfoil

slower moving air

Lift

Roto-copter

This paper roto-copter spins like a tiny helicopter.

Why does it spin? As the roto-copter falls, air pushes up against the rotor blades, bending them slightly. As the blades bend, some of the upward thrust becomes a sideways push. Since the "push" from each blade pushes in the opposite direction, this makes the roto-copter spin, rather than move sideways.

To make the roto-copter, you will need:
- sheet of construction paper, 7 inches x 3.5 inches (18 cm x 9 cm)
- pencil • ruler
- scissors
- paper clip

1

solid line

2.4 inches (6 cm)

1.8 inches (4.5 cm)

3 cm

1.8 inches (4.5 cm)

solid line

3.5 inches (9 cm)

1.2 inches (3 cm)

1.2 inches (3 cm)

1.2 inches (3 cm)

solid line

Draw solid and dotted lines on the sheet of paper. Cut along the solid lines.

2

Fold the top right strip down along the dotted line. Crease along the fold.

3

Turn the paper over. Fold the top right strip down level with the fold of the first strip. Crease along the fold.

4

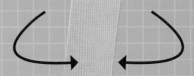

Open out the folds at the top. Fold along the two vertical dotted lines, folding the paper into the middle to form a stem.

5

Fold up about 1 inch (2.5 cm) of the paper stem at the base of the roto-copter. Slide the paper clip on.

stem

Try this!
Open out the paper and use crayons or felt-tip pens to decorate your roto-copter. Fold it back into shape. What happens to the colors when the roto-copter spins?

SAFETY FIRST
Ask an adult to supervise when you launch your roto-copter. Be careful if standing on a staircase. Ask an adult to launch the roto-copter from a first-floor window. Stretch your arm out to drop the roto-copter away from your body.

To launch the roto-copter, you will need:
- something solid to stand on, such as a staircase, OR ask an adult to launch the roto-copter from a first-floor window
- paper and pen to record your findings

6

Hold the roto-copter away from your body by the stem above the paper clip and throw it into the air. Watch it spin to the ground!

A fair test
Try making these adjustments to the roto-copter. Only change one thing at a time, and record what happens.
- How does it affect the flight if you make a bigger roto-copter?
- What happens if you change the length of the roto-copter blades?
- What happens if you use a heavier paper clip?
- Does it make a difference if you use thicker paper?

Whirligig

Watch this spinning whirligig whizz through the air!

How does it work? As the whirligig falls, air pushes up against its blades but also pushes sideways on them. This makes the whirligig spin around and move sideways through the air.

To make the whirligig, you will need:
- wooden craft stick
- dish containing warm water
- paint and paintbrush
- hot glue gun
- pencil

1

Put the craft stick into a dish of warm water. Leave it for an hour.

2 Hold both ends of the stick between your finger and thumb. Gently twist one end toward you and the other end away from you, until the craft stick stays twisted when you let go. Leave to dry.

SAFETY FIRST
Ask an adult to supervise when you use the hot glue gun.

3

Paint the craft stick. Leave to dry.

Use the hot glue gun to put a blob of glue on the flat end of the pencil. Place it in the center of the craft stick. Hold it in place until it cools (this will only take a few seconds).

4

With your hands pressed together, hold the pencil between the fingers of your right hand and the palm of your left hand. Very quickly pull back your left hand and push forward your right hand. The whirligig will shoot off, spinning as it goes.

11

The hammer glider

Turn a sheet of paper into an awesome flying machine!

How does the hammer glider fly? When you throw the glider into the air, the force you use creates thrust. The force that keeps it in the air is called lift. To find out about lift and thrust, see page 8.

To make the hammer glider, you will need:
- letter-sized sheet of thin paper
- ruler
- decorative craft tape
- scissors

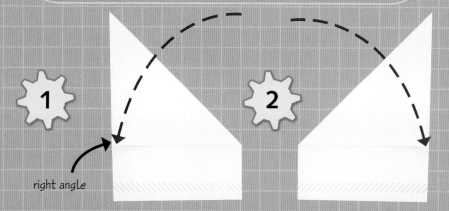

1

right angle

Attach a piece of craft tape 1 inch (2.5 cm) from the bottom of both sides of the sheet of paper. Fold the right-hand corner down at a right angle. Crease and unfold.

2

Fold the left-hand corner down at a right angle. Crease and unfold.

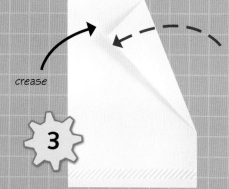

crease

3

Fold the top right corner down so that the long edge rests along the diagonal crease.

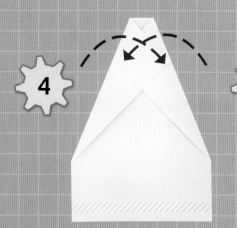

4

Fold the top left corner down so that the long edge rests along the other diagonal crease.

5

Fold the paper in half. Crease and unfold.

6

Fold the top down to the bottom edge. Match up the edges. Crease along the fold.

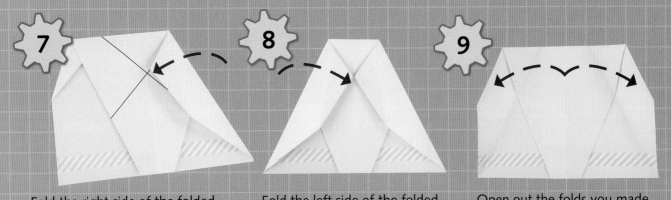

7 Fold the right side of the folded paper to where the crease lines form a cross. Crease along the fold.

8 Fold the left side of the folded paper in the same way. Crease along the fold.

9 Open out the folds you made in steps 7 and 8.

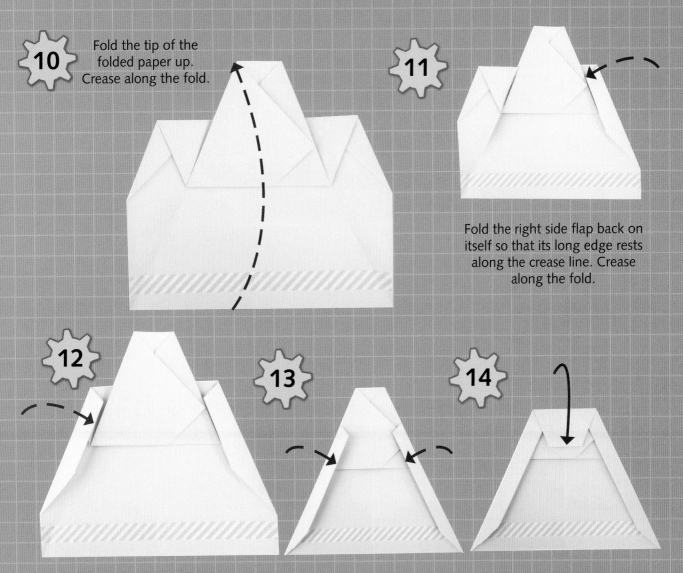

10 Fold the tip of the folded paper up. Crease along the fold.

11 Fold the right side flap back on itself so that its long edge rests along the crease line. Crease along the fold.

12 Repeat step 11 on the left side.

13 Fold both sides over once more, along the crease lines. Crease along the folds.

14 Fold the top down. Crease along the fold.

15

Fold

Fold both sides together along the crease that runs along the length of what will be the glider's body, with the flaps on the outside.

16

Fold one wing down so that its edge meets up with the central fold. Crease along the fold.

17

Turn over. Fold the second wing down so that its edge meets up with the central fold. Open out the glider.

To launch the hammer glider, you will need:
- an open space

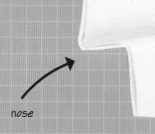

SAFETY FIRST

Even simple paper gliders can be dangerous. Find an open space where you are in no danger of hitting anyone.
Aim the glider at a specific point.

nose

18

Hold the glider gently, with your finger and thumb on either side of the central fold. Pull back your hand and launch the glider into the air in front of you, with the nose pointing slightly upward.

How to fly a plane

Flying a plane

A pilot uses cockpit controls to move parts of the plane to change direction.

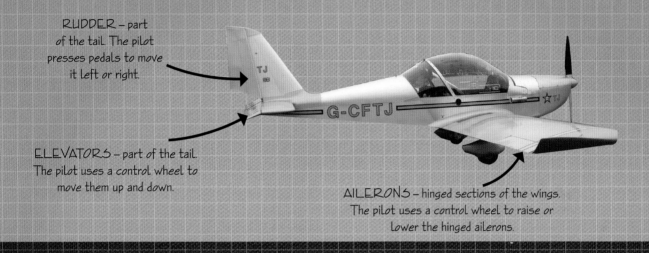

RUDDER – part of the tail. The pilot presses pedals to move it left or right.

ELEVATORS – part of the tail. The pilot uses a control wheel to move them up and down.

AILERONS – hinged sections of the wings. The pilot uses a control wheel to raise or lower the hinged ailerons.

To fly an aircraft straight and level, a pilot controls three types of movement:

Pitch: rotation around the side-to-side **axis**. The pilot raises or lowers the elevators on the tail piece to control pitch. By controlling the pitch of the plane, the pilot makes the plane **ascend** or **descend**.

Yaw: rotation around the **vertical** axis. The pilot moves the rudder to the left or the right to control the yaw. By moving the rudder and the ailerons, the pilot turns the plane.

Roll: rotation around the **horizontal** axis. By raising or lowering the ailerons on the wings, the pilot makes the plane roll to the left or right, which helps to turn the plane.

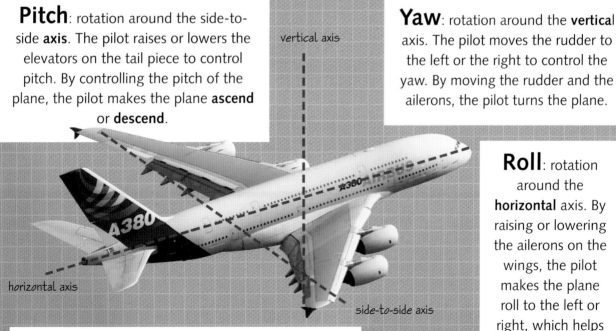

vertical axis

horizontal axis

side-to-side axis

To see animations of these movements visit:
www.grc.nasa.gov/www/k-12/airplane/roll.html
www.grc.nasa.gov/www/k-12/airplane/yaw.html
www.grc.nasa.gov/www/k-12/airplane/pitch.html

15

Bernoulli glider

See Bernoulli's Principle in action with this paper glider.

This glider's wings form an airfoil. The air moving over the curved top travels a little faster than the air traveling underneath the glider. This creates lower air pressure above the wings and higher air pressure beneath the wings, leading to lift, which pushes the glider up into the air.

To make a Bernoulli glider, you will need:
- pencil and thin white paper (for tracing the template)
- letter-sized sheet of thick wrapping paper
- scissors
- double-sided tape

1

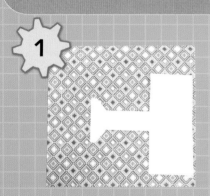

Use the pencil and thin white paper to trace the template on page 29. Cut it out and draw around it on the wrapping paper.

2

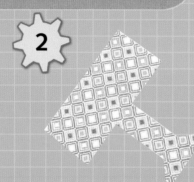

Cut out the paper glider shape.

3

fold and crease

Fold the glider shape in half lengthwise. Crease and unfold.

4

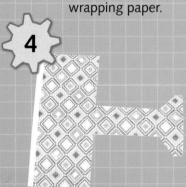

Stick a thin strip of double-sided tape along the front edge. Peel off the backing paper.

5

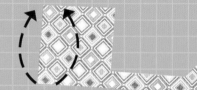

X

X

Fold the front edge back on itself but DO NOT crease along the fold. Press the two edges together between the points marked X, attaching them together along the length of the double-sided tape.

6

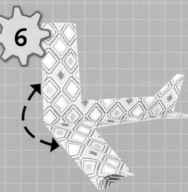

Fold the glider in half along its length. Open it out, keeping a semi-folded shape.

To launch the Bernoulli glider, you will need:

- an open space
- paper and pen to record what happens

7 Hold the glider lightly underneath, between your thumb and finger. Launch the glider into the air in front of you with the nose pointing slightly upward.

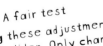

A fair test

Try making these adjustments to the Bernoulli glider. Only change one thing at a time, and record what happens.

- What happens if you add a small blob of sticky tack to the nose of the glider?
- How does the glider fly if you make four cuts in the tail and fold the tail up to form two flaps?

For more about Bernoulli's Principle, turn to page 8.

If you make adjustments to the way the glider flies (see left), you will see the effects that a pilot can make on an airplane's flight by using some of the cockpit controls (see page 15 for more on this).

17

Catapult glider

Use rubber bands to catapult this glider into the air.

How does this work? The glider is made from light materials that make it stay airborne. It is launched into the air with the thrust from the energy stored in the rubber bands.

To make the catapult glider, you will need:
- pencil and thin white paper (for tracing the template)
- letter-size sheet construction paper
- scissors
- straight drinking straw
- 2 long rubber bands
- stapler

1

Trace the template on page 28 and use it to cut out one wing and two tail pieces from the construction paper.

2

Fold the wing piece along the center, unfold it, and place it on top of the drinking straw. Loop the rubber band under the drinking straw at the back of the wing.

3

Pull the free loop of the rubber band over the paper wing and loop it around the drinking straw at the other side of the wing.

4

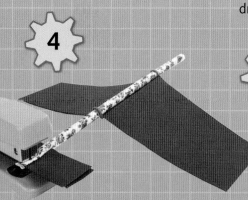

Turn it over and use the scissors to make a horizontal cut in the end of the drinking straw. Slide in the tail pieces. Staple them in place. Turn it over. Bend the wings up around the drinking straw.

5

Fold the top tail piece up around the drinking straw.

6

Push the end of the second rubber band into the end of the drinking straw at the nose of the glider. Staple it in place.

18

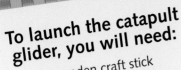

To launch the catapult glider, you will need:

- wooden craft stick
(ask an adult to cut a small notch out of one end)
- paper and pen to record what happens

7

Hook the elastic band at the front of the glider into the notch in the craft stick. Hold the glider between the wing and the tail. Point the glider's nose up into the air.

8 Pull back on the glider. Let go and watch it catapult into the air!

A fair test

Try making these adjustments to the catapult glider. Only make one change at a time, and record what happens.

- Try changing the shape of the wings.
- What happens if you slide the wings backward?
- What happens if you slide the wings forward?
- Try using thinner paper.

Glitch Fix!

Glitch: the glider nose dives.
Fix: find the center of gravity by placing the drinking straw part of the glider on your fingertip. Slide the wings backward or forward until the glider balances.

Rubber band helicopter

Create a working helicopter using a propeller and a rubber band.

How does it work? Energy is stored in the rubber band by winding the propeller. When the helicopter is launched, the rubber band releases energy, which turns the propeller. As the propeller spins it pushes air behind it, which pulls the helicopter forward.

To make the rubber band helicopter, you will need:
- 7-inch (18 cm) hook nose propeller (available from hobby or craft stores)
- wood craft stick (sized to attach snugly to propeller)
- paper clip
- duct tape
- pencil and thin white paper (for tracing the template)
- long elastic band
- construction paper
- glue and spreader

1
Slide the propeller onto the end of the wood stick.

2
Bend the paper clip.

3
Place it on the other end of the wood stick.

4
Use duct tape to attach the paper clip where it touches the wood stick.

5
Loop one end of the rubber band onto the hook under the propeller.

hook

6

Hook the other end of the rubber band onto the paper clip.

7

Using the template on page 28, trace and cut out the helicopter shape with construction paper.

8

Tape the paper helicopter shape onto the wood stick on the side opposite to the propeller hook.

Turn the propeller clockwise 50 times to twist the rubber band. Move to step 9.

To launch the rubber band helicopter, you will need:
- an open space
- paper and pen to record what happens

9

Hold the propeller and rubber band firmly until you are ready to fly the helicopter. Let go of the propeller and the rubber band.

SAFETY FIRST

Even simple rubber-band-powered helicopters can be dangerous. Find an open space where you are in no danger of hitting anyone.

Rubber band plane

Made carefully, this plane can soar high into the sky!

How does it work? Energy is stored in the rubber band by winding the propeller. When you let go of the propeller, the rubber band releases its stored energy, which turns the propeller. As the propeller spins, it pushes air backward and the airplane flies forward. The light materials used to make this plane help it stay in the air and defy gravity.

To make the rubber band plane, you will need:
- 6-inch (15 cm) hook nose propeller (available from hobby or craft stores)
- wooden craft stick (sized to attach snugly to propeller)
- long rubber band
- paper clip
- pliers • ruler
- pencil and 2 sheets of thin white paper (for tracing the templates)
- large sheet of tissue paper
- masking tape
- glue stick
- package of wood craft sticks
- hot glue gun
- felt-tip pen
- 4 toothpicks
- scissors

1

Attach the wood craft stick to the propeller.

2

Place the ends of the rubber band together and tie them in a knot. Slide the knot along the rubber band to the end to create a big loop.

3

SAFETY FIRST
Ask an adult to supervise when you use the pliers.

Open out the paper clip.
Use pliers to cut off 1 inch (2.5 cm) on one end and bend the other end.

4

5

Loop the rubber band over the hook on the propeller. Pull on the knotted end of the rubber band until the band is straight but not over stretched. Make a pencil mark on the craft stick, just above the knot.

Push the straight end of the paper clip into the craft stick where you made the mark. Use the hot glue gun to hold it in place, with the bent part angled away from the propeller. Leave it to dry. Loop over the knotted end of the rubber band. Set to one side.

6

Use the thin white paper to trace the templates on pages 28 and 29. Cut a piece of tissue paper and use masking tape to tape it in place on top of the traced templates.

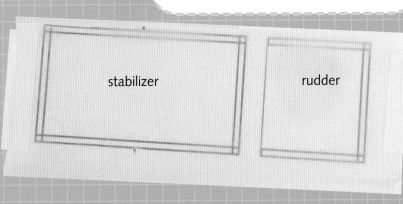

stabilizer

rudder

7

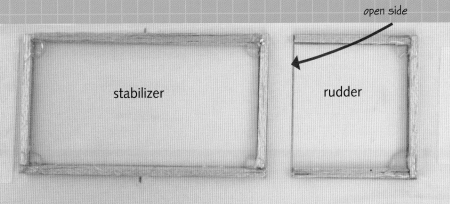

stabilizer

rudder

open side

Use scissors to cut four pieces of the wooden craft sticks to fit along the edges of the **stabilizer** piece. Glue the craft stick onto the tissue paper using the glue stick. Make sure the ends touch at the corners. Use a blob of hot glue to join the corners. Leave to set.

Use scissors to cut three pieces of craft sticks to fit the top edge, right side, and bottom edge of the rudder section. Glue the craft sticks onto the tissue paper using the glue stick. Make sure the ends touch at the corners. Use a blob of hot glue to join the corners. Leave to set.

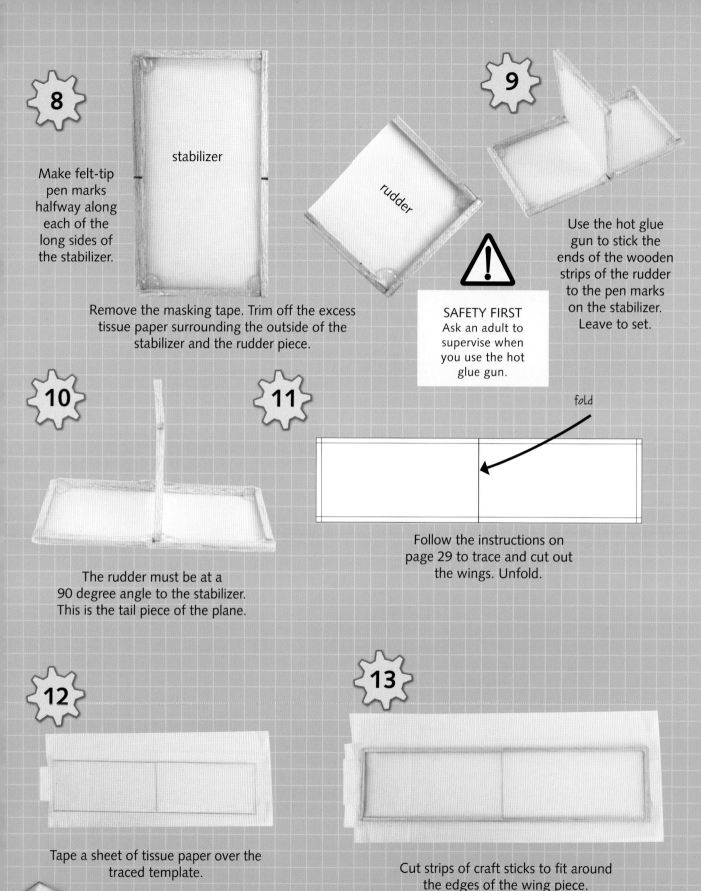

8

stabilizer

Make felt-tip pen marks halfway along each of the long sides of the stabilizer.

Remove the masking tape. Trim off the excess tissue paper surrounding the outside of the stabilizer and the rudder piece.

rudder

9

Use the hot glue gun to stick the ends of the wooden strips of the rudder to the pen marks on the stabilizer. Leave to set.

SAFETY FIRST
Ask an adult to supervise when you use the hot glue gun.

10

The rudder must be at a 90 degree angle to the stabilizer. This is the tail piece of the plane.

11

fold

Follow the instructions on page 29 to trace and cut out the wings. Unfold.

12

Tape a sheet of tissue paper over the traced template.

13

Cut strips of craft sticks to fit around the edges of the wing piece.

24

Use the glue stick to attach the craft sticks onto the tissue paper. Make sure the ends touch at the corners.

Use a blob of hot glue to join the corners. Leave to set.

Use a felt-tip pen to mark the wood at the center of the long sides of the wing piece.

17

Remove the masking tape. Trim away the excess tissue paper.

3.9-inch (10 cm)
Length of craft stick

3 inches (7.5 cm)

18

With the wood strips on the outside, carefully bend the wings at the halfway marks. Prop the wing piece up on a table so that the highest point is 3 inches (7.5 cm) above the table. Attach a 3.9-inch (10 cm) length of craft stick across the center of the wing using the hot glue gun. It will overhang a bit on each side.

19

Use scissors to cut the sharp points off the toothpicks.

20

Use the hot glue gun to attach a toothpick to each side of the central strip of wood. Leave to dry.

21

With the elastic band under the wooden body of the plane, called the fuselage, use the hot glue gun to attach the tail piece you completed in step 10. Only glue the wood, not the tissue paper. Leave to dry.

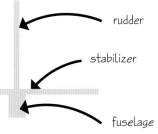

rudder

stabilizer

fuselage

When you view the plane from the back, the rudder and stabilizer should be in line with the end of the fuselage.

22

Use the hot glue gun to stick two of the toothpicks that form part of the wing piece on either side of the fuselage, about 3 inches (7.5 cm) from the propeller.

Now glue the back two toothpicks on the wing section so that they end about 0.5 inches (1.27 cm) below the fuselage. This means that the wings will be angled, which will aid flight.

26

To launch the rubber-band plane, you will need:

- plenty of space
- a stopwatch (and a friend to use it)
- paper and pen to record what happens

23

Wind the propeller clockwise 50 times to twist the rubber band.

24

Hold the plane up in the air. Ask a friend to be ready to press the stopwatch the moment you launch the plane and stop it when the plane lands. Let go of the propeller and watch the test flight. Record the length of the flight.

A fair test

Try making these adjustments to the rubber band plane. Only make one change at a time, and record what happens.

- What happens if you make more turns on the rubber band?
- What happens if you try to wind the propeller the other way?

Templates

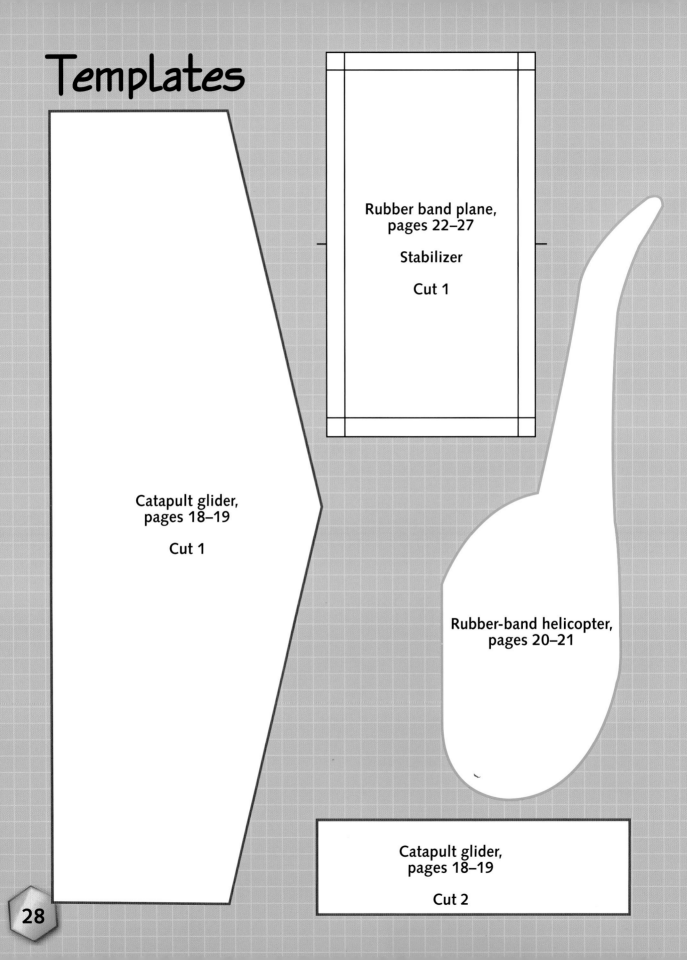

Rubber band plane,
pages 22–27

Stabilizer

Cut 1

Catapult glider,
pages 18–19

Cut 1

Rubber-band helicopter,
pages 20–21

Catapult glider,
pages 18–19

Cut 2

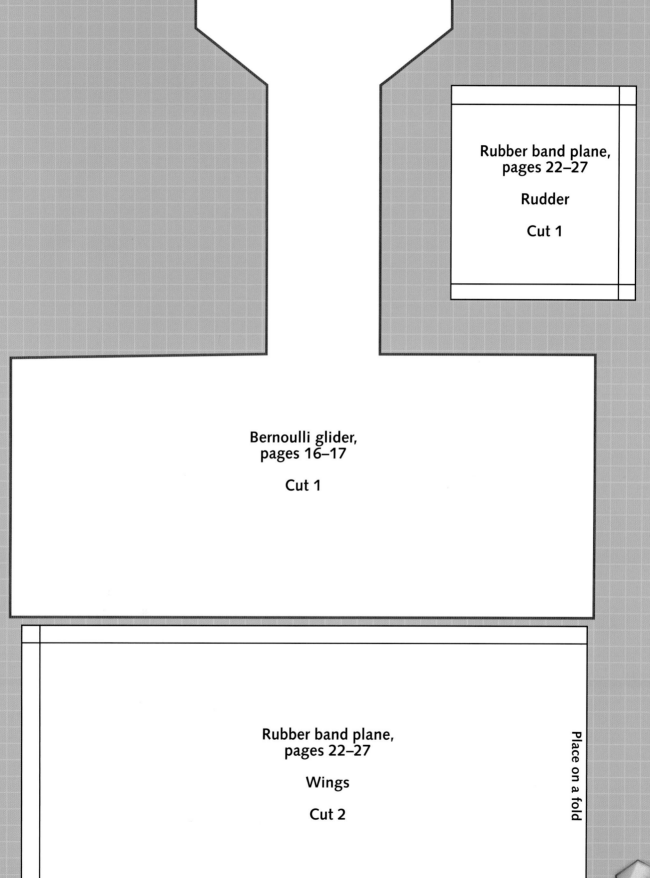

Rubber band plane,
pages 22–27

Rudder

Cut 1

Bernoulli glider,
pages 16–17

Cut 1

Rubber band plane,
pages 22–27

Wings

Cut 2

Place on a fold

Aircraft timeline

The Italian artist, Leonardo da Vinci, was fascinated by flight. In 1485, he made several drawings of flying machines, including winged devices and a human-powered flying machine.

1485

The first hot-air balloon was invented by Joseph-Michel and Jacques-Étienne Montgolfier. The balloon was powered by hot air generated by a fire beneath the basket. The first flight rose 3,280 feet (1,000 m) into the air, while the second flight carried a sheep, a duck, and a rooster on a flight that lasted eight minutes. The same year, Jean-François Pilâtre de Rozier and François Laurent were the first passengers, but this time the balloon was tied to the ground.

1783

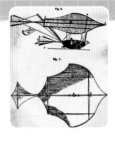

Sir George Cayley, an English engineer, was sometimes known as the *"father of aviation."* He identified the four forces that act on an airplane in flight – lift, drag, thrust, and gravity (see page 8). He recognized that an airplane would need power to keep it in the air for any length of time. In 1853, his coachman, John Appleby, made the first manned glider flight in a glider designed by Cayley.

1853

1891–1896

Otto Lilienthal, a German engineer, designed the first glider capable of carrying a person and flying a long distance. His studied bird flight, conducted experiments, and published his results in 1889. This book was used by the Wright brothers (see below left). His glider was similar to a modern hang glider, with a bar to hang on to.

Alberto Santos-Dumont, a Brazilian pilot, won the Aero Club of France's prize in 1901. He successfully circled the Eiffel Tower and returned to his starting point in less than 30 minutes in the airship he designed.

1901

The first powered airplane flight occurred in 1903 at Kitty Hawk, North Carolina. Orville and Wilbur Wright had been designing and testing gliders since 1899. In 1903 they added an engine to their best design and the *Flyer* made a 12-second flight on 17 December. By late 1905, their third powered airplane could make flights that lasted several minutes.

1903

1927

Charles Lindbergh completed the first solo, non-stop trans-Atlantic flight. He flew from New York, to Paris, France.

1932

Frank Whittle, an engineer and pilot, was granted the first **patent** for a jet engine in 1932. The first jet aircraft with a Whittle engine flew in 1939.

1932

Amelia Earhart was the first woman to make a solo non-stop trans-Atlantic flight.

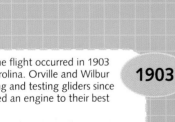

The Concorde jet carried passengers on **supersonic** flights, cutting journey times in half. The Concorde broke the sound barrier, causing noise pollution in the form of a **sonic boom**.

1976–2003

Today

We take flight travel for granted. Approximately 100,000 passenger flights occur every day, and goods are easily shipped by plane to different countries around the world.

Glossary

Please note: Some boldfaced words are defined where they appear in the text.

airborne To be up in the air

ascend To climb upward

axis The center around which something rotates

catapult To use a machine to help launch things into the air

descend To move downward

forces The push or pull motion that acts on an object

friction A force that slows down movement when one surface slides over another

glider A type of flying machine without an engine

horizontal A line which runs across from left to right

hypersonic To move at five or more times the speed of sound, also called Mach 5

lift The upward force produced on a wing when it moves through the air

patent A license granting the sole right for a set period of time to make, use, or sell an invention

reconnaissance A military mission to gather information about an enemy

sonic boom A loud noise that occurs when an object travels faster than the speed of sound. This is also known as breaking the sound barrier

stabilizer A section of an airplane designed to give the craft stability and help it fly straight

supersonic To move at up to five times the speed of sound

thrust A pushing force that moves something forward

vertical A line which runs straight up and down

Learning More

Books

Mercer, Bobby. *The Flying Machine Book: Build and Launch 35 Rockets, Gliders, Helicopters, Boomerangs, and More*. Chicago Review Press, 2012.

Rooney, Anne. *Aerospace Engineering and the Principles of Flight*. Crabtree Publishing, 2013.

Spilsbury, Richard. *Great Aircraft Designs: 1900–Today*. Heinemann Educational Books, 2015.

Websites

Discover how to build the world record-holding paper plane here:
www.aviation-for-kids.com/paper-airplanes.html

Escape the jungle by building your own plane:
www.nms.ac.uk/explore/play/plane-builder/

Learn more about the principles of flight here:
www.grc.nasa.gov/WWW/K-12/UEET/StudentSite/aeronautics.html

Index